SHE SPEAKS

A COLLECTION OF WOMEN'S EMPOWERING SPEECHES

DR. JAGADEESH PILLAI

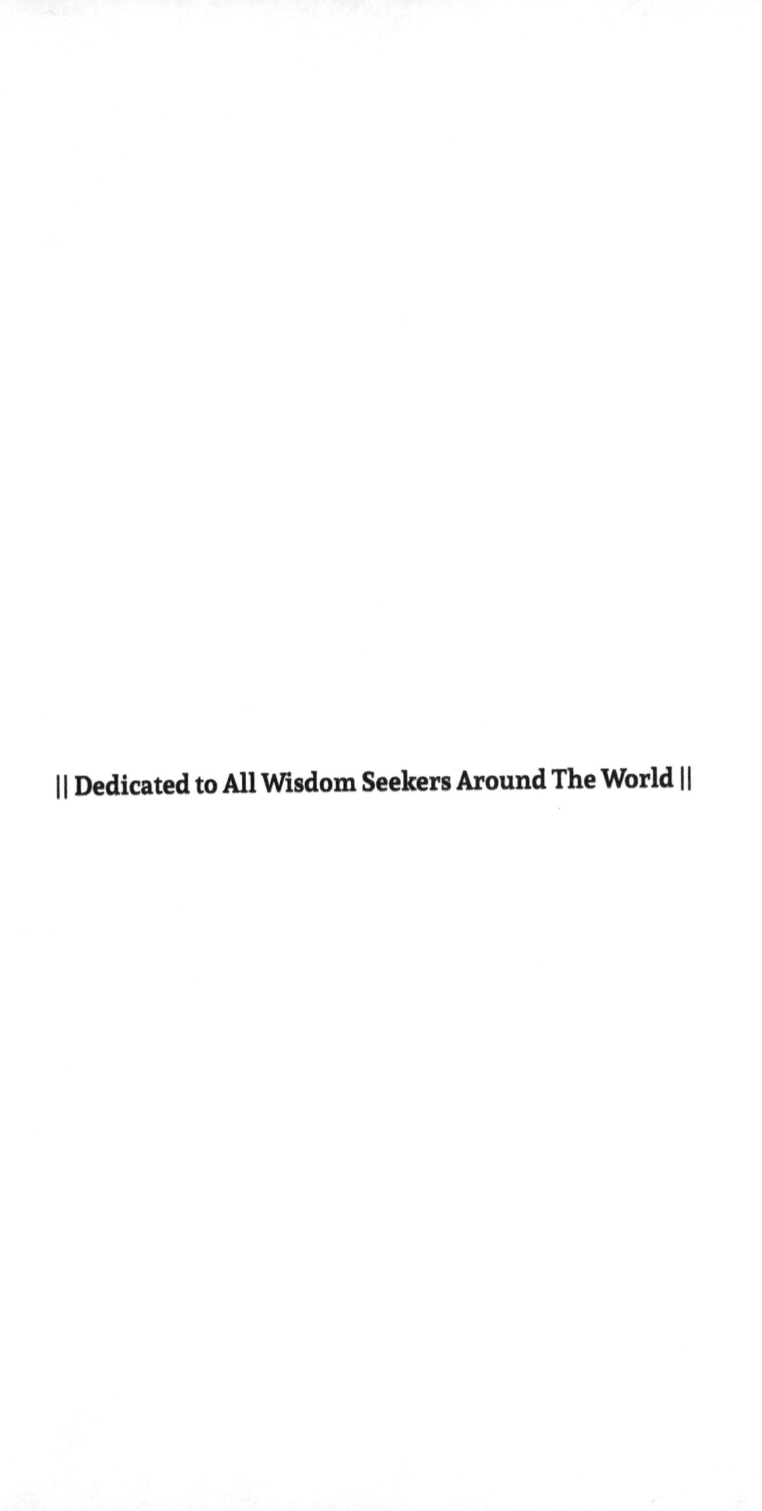

|| Dedicated to All Wisdom Seekers Around The World ||

Contents

Prayer — vii

About The Author — ix

Preface — xiii

1. Aung San Suu Kyi (myanmar) — 1

2. Melinda Gates — 4

3. Gloria Steinem — 6

4. Ruth Bader Ginsburg — 8

5. Emma González — 11

6. Angela Davis — 13

7. Sheryl Sandberg — 16

8. Oprah Winfrey — 19

9. Irom Sharmila Chanu — 21

10. Tawakkol Karman — 23

11. Rigoberta Menchú — 26

12. Wangari Maathai — 29

13. Malala Yousafzai — 31

14. Mother Teresa — 33

15. Hillary Clinton — 36

16. Emma Watson — 38

17. Chimamanda Ngozi Adichie — 41

18. Isabel Allende — 44

19. Mary Robinson — 47

Other Books Of The Author — 49

Contact — 53

Prayer

**"Om Poornamadah Poornamidam Poornat
Poornamudachyate,Poornasya Poornamaadaya
Poornamevavashishyate,Om Shantih, Shantih, Shantih"**

*The literal interpretation of this mantra is: That which is
Absolute, This which is Absolute, Absolute arises from Absolute,
If Absolute is removed from Absolute, Absolute remains
OM Peace, Peace, Peace.*

About the Author

Dr. Jagadeesh Pillai is a renowned Guinness World Record holder, writer, and researcher hailing from Varanasi, also known as the abode of Lord Shiva. With a Ph.D. in Vedic Science and a range of creative ideas and achievements, he is a true polymath. He is the author of more than 100 books including Research Publications. Although his roots can be traced back to Kerala, the people of Varanasi hold him in high regard and affectionately consider him one of their own.

Dr. Pillai has achieved four Guinness World Records in the following subjects:

1. "Script to Screen" - In this record, Dr. Pillai produced and directed an animation film within the shortest time possible, breaking the previous record set by Canadians. He has also received numerous national and international awards and recognitions for this achievement.

2. Longest Line of Postcards - For this record, Dr. Pillai created a line of 16,300 postcards on the occasion of the 163rd anniversary of Indian Postal Day. The event also included a questionnaire about the Indian flag.

3. Largest Poster Awareness Campaign - Dr. Pillai designed an awareness campaign on the subject of "Beti Bachao - Beti Padhao" (Save the Girl Child - Educate the Girl Child)

to achieve this record.

4. Largest Envelope - In tribute to the Indian Prime Minister's "Make in India" initiative, Dr. Pillai created a 4000 square meter envelope using waste paper to achieve this record.

5. Attempted - 70000 Candles on a 210 kg Cake - To celebrate the 70th Indian Independence Day, Dr. Pillai attempted to light 70,000 candles on a 210 kg cake, which was recorded in World Records India.

6. Attempted - Documentary on Dhamek Stupa of Sarnath in 17 Languages - Dr. Pillai attempted to create a documentary on the Dhamek Stupa of Sarnath, dubbing it in 17 different languages. The result of this attempt is currently awaiting confirmation from the Guinness World Records.

Dr. Pillai is skilled in teaching the Bhagavad Gita, a Hindu scripture, and is popular among young people. He has helped many young people improve their lives through his motivational teachings.

In addition to teaching, he has composed and sung numerous Sanskrit Bhajans and patriotic songs.

He has also written and directed several short films and documentaries for awareness campaigns, and has volunteered with the police in both UP and Kerala to spread awareness about various issues through videos and photography.

He has a goal of writing thousands of books on Indian culture, Indian temples, and the lives of extraordinary people. Incredibly, he has produced and directed over 100 documentaries about the city of Varanasi, all on his own.

He has also helped and guided more than 25 boys and girls to achieve world records through creative and innovative methods. He is a multifaceted person who uses his intellect and the blessings given to him by God to excel in various areas. He is both a teacher and a student, always learning and teaching, and is able to master any subject he comes across.

He is a selfless social activist and motivational speaker who has overcome struggles and failures to become a successful and enthusiastic individual with a rich life experience.

In addition to his work with the Bhagavad Gita, he is also an efficient Tarot card reader, Astro-Vastu consultant, and a talented singer and composer. He has sung the entire Ram Charita Manas and Bhagavad Gita in his own compositions, and has sung the phrase "Lokah Samastha Sukhino Bhavantu" in 50 different languages. He is currently working on a detailed and scientific study of Vedas, Upanishads, Puranas, and the Bhagavad Gita. He has also composed and sung the Hanuman Chalisa and Gayatri Mantra in 108 and 1008 different compositions, respectively.

Awards - Four Times Guinness World Records, Winner of Mahatma Gandhi Vishwa Shanti Puraskar , Mahatma Gandhi Global Peace Ambassador, Kashi Ratna Award, Dr. APJ Abdul Kalam Motivational Person of the Year 2017, Mother Teresa Award, Indira Gandhi Priyadarshini Award, Bharat Vikas Ratna Award, Udyog Ratna Award, Vigyan Prasar Award, Poorvanchal Ratn Samman.

PREFACE

In this book, we have collected a selection of speeches given by women from around the world that have had a profound impact on people and society. These speeches represent a wide range of perspectives and experiences, but they all share one thing in common: they were delivered by women who were determined to make a difference.

Throughout history, women's voices have too often been silenced, marginalized, or overlooked. But these speeches demonstrate that when women speak up, they can change the world. They can inspire movements, challenge injustice, and empower others. They can make people think, feel, and take action.

The speeches in this book cover a wide variety of subjects, from human rights and social justice to education and climate change. They were given in different contexts and at different times, but they all have relevance today. They remind us that the struggles for equality and freedom are ongoing, and that we have much to learn from those who came before us.

Reading this book, you'll find speeches of women who have faced oppression, discrimination, and violence, but who have not let it stop them from fighting for their beliefs. You'll also find speeches of women who have achieved great things, and have become role models for others. Their speeches will show you the power of words, the importance of courage, and the potential of individuals to make a difference.

This book is not only about speeches, but about the stories of women who stood up, spoke out, and changed the world. Their speeches will inspire you to be a better person, to stand up for what you believe in and to make a change in your own way.

Through these speeches, we can learn from these women's experiences, acknowledge the issues they have spoken about and appreciate the work they have done, even if they have given their speeches decades ago, their messages are still applicable and relevant today.

I

Aung San Suu Kyi (Myanmar)

Aung San Suu Kyi (Myanmar) - pro-democracy leader and Nobel Peace Prize winner.

Aung San Suu Kyi is a Nobel Peace Prize laureate who has had a profound impact on the people of Myanmar. Born in Yangon in 1945, she is the eldest child of two democracy activists, Aung San and Khin Kyi. She studied in Myanmar and later went on to Oxford University in the United Kingdom, where she received her degree in philosophy, politics, and economics. After a period of political exile, she returned to Myanmar in 1988 in response to the uprisings against the military junta who had been in power since 1962.

Upon her return, Suu Kyi became the leader of the democracy movement. As the time she wrote articles and gave speeches in various parts of the country, often in defiance of the authorities. She reiterated that the people should remain peaceful and continue to work for what they believed in. In 1991, Suu Kyi was awarded the Nobel Peace Prize, despite her house arrest since 1989.

Even during her house arrest, Suu Kyi continued her dedication to democracy. She would often hold press conferences for foreign media, in which she expressed her commitment to non-violent methods and her rejection of armed struggle. She continued to deliver powerful speeches, despite her imprisonment and threats from the government.

In May 2012, Suu Kyi was elected to the Parliament, a major accomplishment after her long struggle for democracy in Myanmar. She has continued to speak out for the rights of human rights and politically activist citizens; her speeches now draw thousands of supporters. In a speech delivered to the United Nations in 2013, Suu Kyi said, "We must strive to be a nation of unwavering justice, equality and human rights."

Suu Kyi can also be credited with a great deal of reform in Myanmar. She has continued to fight for democratic reform and worked closely with members of the press to ensure that the people are provided with accurate news and information. She has worked hard to ensure that Myanmar citizens have access to decent education and healthcare, and she has pressed for reduced corruption and inequality within the country.

Aung San Suu Kyi's speeches have inspired millions of people across the world. Today her legacy continues to live on; she is seen as an example of perseverance and dedication. Her commitment to democracy and improvement of human rights in Myanmar remain an inspiration for many to fight for what they believe in. Though there is still much progress to be made, her words have conveyed her unwavering belief that one person can make a difference.

II

Melinda Gates

Melinda Gates, a philanthropist and advocate, has been a tireless promoter of the empowerment of women and girls, technical literacy and global health. Her speech inspiringly captures the impact of investment in global education and accessibility of health care as well as her personal journey.

Gates's speech is mainly focused on how everyone must strive to redirect public and private funding towards the development and education of girls and women. She shares how she has used the Bill and Melinda Gates Foundation to champion gender equality in the past two decades. She claims that gender equality isn't just right idea, but it's an investment in the future. By directly investing in the empowerment of women and girls, they believe they can build a stronger global future.

Moreover, Gates elaborates on her aspiration to make sure that every person can access to quality education resources, highlighting the importance of investment in digital technology and digital education as well. According to

Gates, increasing global access to digital education can lead to improved college enrollment, job skills and career paths. She shares her personal experiences and successes, with an emphasis on her emotional journey around education and technology.

The speech furthermore emphasizes the importance of health care and the need for improved accessibility. Gates shares that she firmly believes that good health — strong communities, families and economies — is the fundamental foundation of a good life. Gates shares her experience that health is brought to a community starts with the individual – and in order to create positive change, each of us needs to be responsible for our health.

By focusing on the power and potential of investment in education and improved accessibility to health care, Gates emphasized that in order to make a difference, resources must be invested in the right places. It's crucial to focus on what works, move beyond traditional methods, and support the creative solutions people come up with.

Gates's speech is highly motivating and inspiring. With her vision, commitment and ongoing work in the areas of global education and health care, she has the potential to create far-reaching and lasting progress.

III

Gloria Steinem

Gloria Steinem (United States) - feminist and civil rights activist.

Gloria Steinem is an iconic figure in the feminist and civil rights movements who has been championing for greater gender and racial equality for over fifty years. She has made profound and lasting contributions to the social and political changes that have taken place in the last half century, and her words continue to shape the current public discourse surrounding issues of gender and race.

In her lifetime, Steinem has given many effective and influential speeches aimed at inspiring change and challenge outdated norms. One of the most powerful and memorable of these speeches is her 1994 address to the St. Lawrence University Class of 1994, titled "The Politics of Illusion."

In this speech, Steinem addressed the importance of vision and courage in creating a better world. She began by discussing how androcentric societies have grown out of illusions that favor men over women, along with other false constructs of power. She then moved on to discuss the need for an imagination revolution, reimagining and reclaiming a world of freedom and opportunity for all genders, races, and beliefs.

Although primarily a call to action for change, Steinem also highlighted the many successes women have achieved in the face of what often seems like insurmountable opposition. She pointed to the courage of activists and how they are slowly but surely breaking through the boundaries of conformity.

Steinem also touched on the importance of intersectionality and diversity in both public and private spheres. She explained how the full spectrum of humanity must be taken into account if we are to create an accepting, tolerant, and equitable world.

Steinem's speech is an inspiring reminder that it is only through the strength, courage, and determination of individuals and communities that we can create a society of true justice and equality. It is a call to action to challenge injustice and oppression, and to believe in the power of collective voice to create lasting change. Overwhelmingly, her speech is a reminder of the importance of courage in the face of the status quo, and of the power of unity for a fairer and more equal tomorrow.

IV

Ruth Bader Ginsburg

Ruth Bader Ginsburg (United States) - Supreme Court Justice and advocate for gender equality.

Ruth Bader Ginsburg was a trailblazer for gender equality and a powerful voice for women's rights during her time as a Supreme Court Justice of the United States. Throughout her career, she fought for equal rights for all citizens, particularly women, and her speeches reflected her unwavering commitment to this cause.

One of her most inspiring speeches was delivered in 1984 at a conference of the International Women's Rights Action Watch. In this speech, she spoke about the urgent need to eradicate gender-based discrimination and the importance of using the law to achieve this goal. She argued that discrimination on the basis of sex was not only unjust, but also a violation of human rights. She said:

"I ask no favor for my sex. All I ask of our brethren is that they take their feet off our necks."

Ginsburg argued that the law should be used as a tool to help women achieve equality, rather than as a tool to discriminate against them. She urged the audience to continue the fight for gender equality, saying that the task was far from complete. She also spoke about the need to change societal attitudes towards women and to educate people about the importance of equality. She stressed that it was not only women who were affected by discrimination, but also men and children, as discrimination limits everyone's potential.

Another speech of hers, in her acceptance to American Bar Association in 2015, she spoke on the need to lift the barriers that were preventing women and minorities from entering the legal profession, and the importance of achieving diversity in the workplace. She said:

"It is not enough to be a good lawyer, or a good judge. It is not enough to be a good human being. Unless we do something about the barriers that impede the progress of women and minorities, progress will be slow and uncertain."

She also discussed the importance of mentorship and role models for young women in the legal profession. Ginsburg highlighted the importance of having diversity of experiences and perspectives on the bench, saying that it leads to better decision making and represents the society better.

Ginsburg's speeches were always filled with her unwavering commitment to achieving gender equality and her belief in the ability of the law to bring about positive change. Her speeches were also marked by her sharp wit and her ability to present complex legal arguments in a clear and persuasive manner.

Throughout her career, Ruth Bader Ginsburg worked tirelessly to promote equal rights and opportunities for women. Her speeches were a powerful reminder of the need to continue this fight and to use the law as a tool to achieve this goal. She has been an inspiration to countless women and continues to be remembered as a strong voice of gender equality and justice.

V

Emma González

Emma González is an inspirational gun control advocate who is well-known for her impassioned speeches and determined activism. Born in the city of Miami, Florida in 1999, González has become world renowned for her leadership in the gun control movement, most notably in the wake of the deadly 2018 mass shooting in Parkland, Florida. In the aftermath of the shooting, González delivered a speech at an anti-gun rally that quickly went viral— garnering millions of views on social media outlets and popularizing her as a gun control advocate.

González's speech focused on the personal loss and grief she experienced as a result of the Parkland shooting, and then shifted to the physical and emotional gravity of gun violence in the US. Beginning her speech with a moment of silence to pay respects to the victims, González poignantly addressed the issue of gun control by declaring, "It's not enough to just allow people to feel safe in their community, we need to make change." This powerful statement highlighted the importance of legislative reform when it comes to effectively tackling gun violence.

González used her speech to call out legislators who receive money from the National Rifle Association and proposed that the only way to affect real change is to vote in politicians who will prioritize gun control more than the financial interests of the NRA. However, the core message of González's speech was her demand: "We call BS." This two-word statement immediately struck a chord with people of all ages and has become a battle-cry among advocates of gun control.

González also launched the National School Walkout movement which saw students across the United States walking out of their classes for seventeen minutes to honor the victims of the Parkland shooting. This action served as both a way to pay tribute to the lives lost and a powerful call for stricter gun control reform.

Emma González's inspiring speech on gun violence will be remembered for generations. Her passionate oration on the issue combined with her willingness to take action has inspired millions of people to fight for stricter gun control legislation. Going forward, we can learn from her determination and her enduring message: "We call BS."

VI

Angela Davis

Angela Davis is a feminist, civil rights activist, and scholar who has made significant contributions to the fight for racial and gender equality in the United States. Throughout her career, she has been a powerful voice for marginalized communities and her speeches reflect her unwavering commitment to social justice.

One of her most inspiring speeches was delivered in 1971 at a meeting of the National Black Feminist Organization. In this speech, she spoke about the intersectionality of race, gender, and class, and how these intersecting oppressions create a distinct experience for black women that cannot be addressed by solely focusing on one aspect of identity. She said:

"We realize that the liberation of all oppressed peoples necessitates the destruction of the political-economic systems of capitalism and imperialism as well as patriarchy. We are socialists because we are here as deliberately women, feminists, and Black people because we are actively committed to redefining those terms. We believe that sexual politics under patriarchy is as pervasive in Black groups as everywhere else in society, and we know that if we who are heterosexual will fight for the rights of homosexuals, who are reflexively oppressed, that we will be able to fight against what is right in front of us."

Davis highlighted the importance of intersectionality and the need to address multiple forms of oppression. She argued that black feminists could not wait for the rest of the movement to catch up, and that it was essential for them to create their own organizations and speak for themselves.

Another speech of hers, in her acceptance to the University of California Santa Cruz in 2018, she spoke on the fight against social inequality and oppression.

She said: "As we continue to organize, to struggle, to fight against all forms of oppression, against racism, sexism, homophobia, transphobia, against capitalism, imperialism and war, against the prison industrial complex, we must remember to center the most marginalized among us."

In her speech, she emphasized the ongoing struggle for justice and the need for people to continue to organize and fight for change. She called for collective action to dismantle systems of oppression and for people to support those who are marginalized and oppressed.

Throughout her career, Angela Davis has been a powerful voice for marginalized communities and has made significant contributions to the fight for racial and gender equality. Her speeches were a call to action, urging people to take a stand against injustice and to fight for social change. Her message continues to be an inspiration to many people and her work continues to be studied, cited and celebrated for its impact on the fight for equality, social justice and human rights.

VII

Sheryl Sandberg

Sheryl Sandberg (United States) - Facebook COO and advocate for women in leadership roles.

On June 1, 2013 Sheryl Sandberg, COO of Facebook and a noted advocate for women's rights, gave a speech at the 2013 Wharton Women in Business Conference. Her speech explored the topic of gender roles and how to create a more equitable workplace.

Sandberg began her speech by drawing attention to the inequality of opportunity and resources between men and women at the workplace. She called attention to the prevalent myth that gender inequalities were no longer an issue, and that the glass ceiling had been shattered. She argued that this was an oversimplification, as "Women are not making it to the top of any profession anywhere in the world." She went on to list countries and their ratios of male to female top business leaders. In the United States, women only make up 5% of the top C-suite leadership positions.

Not only are women currently underrepresented in these higher power positions, but Sandberg also showed how the workplace creates an unequal platform for women to climb the ranks. She argued that the workplace often gives more support and favoritism to men, creating an environment that is unsupportive of female leaders. She also discussed how women are often held to a double-standard and that they are judged more harshly than men.

Sandberg then shifted the focus of her speech, indicating that while current structural inequality creates a difficult environment for women, the individuals themselves need to adjust their personal behaviors and attitudes to create a more equal workplace. She calls this the "leadership revolution," and strongly emphasized that this revolution must include both men and women. She argued that everyone must value the abilities of both genders equally for an equitable workplace to form. To do so, Sandberg showed how it's important for women to recognize and acknowledge their own strengths, and to speak out against gender inequality, rather than silencing themselves.

To close her speech, Sandberg issued a challenge to the audience, encouraging everyone to support and empower women in their professional fields. She argued that if women work together with men to make use of their natural abilities, then "Together we can create a world where the great technological accomplishment of our time is reaching its full potential."

Sheryl Sandberg's speech at the 2013 Wharton Women in Business Conference was a powerful and inspiring message, calling attention to the structural inequality of opportunity and resources between men and women in the workplace. In her speech, Sandberg issued a challenge to the audience, emphasizing the need for a 'leadership revolution' to create more equal workplace. Sandberg argued that a supportive and equal environment could enable more women to reach the highest levels of success.

VIII

Oprah Winfrey

Oprah Winfrey is a media mogul and philanthropist who has had a significant impact on the entertainment industry and popular culture. She has been an influential figure in the United States and her speeches reflect her passion for personal growth, education, and philanthropy.

One of her most inspiring speeches was delivered in 2011 at the The Golden Globe awards ceremony. In this speech, she accepted the Cecil B. DeMille award for lifetime achievement in entertainment. She spoke about her humble beginnings, her rise to fame and the power of perseverance in overcoming adversity. She said:

"I know that every one of us has inside of us the capacity for greatness. It just takes some of us longer to find it than others. But when you do, it is the most powerful thing you will ever experience."

She spoke about the importance of living one's best life, of not giving up on one's dreams, and of the power of the human spirit to overcome obstacles. She encouraged her audience to embrace their struggles as opportunities for growth, and to look for the opportunities in life to fulfill their purpose.

Another speech of hers, in her 2018 acceptance speech for the Robert F. Kennedy Human Rights Ripple of Hope award, she spoke about the power of empathy, compassion, and social responsibility. She said:

"I'm here to remind you that the power of one person can change the world and make it a better place. This idea that one person can make a difference is not a cliche, it's a fact."

She spoke about the importance of using one's platform, resources, and influence to create positive change in the world, and urged the audience to use their power to make a difference in the world.

Throughout her career, Oprah Winfrey has been a powerful voice for personal development, education, and philanthropy. Her speeches were filled with hope, inspiration and the message of never giving up on one's dreams. She has used her own life's journey to demonstrate the power of perseverance, hard work and the human spirit to overcome adversity. She continues to be a role model, an inspiration to many people and her work continues to be celebrated for its impact on many lives, and to society as a whole.

IX

Irom Sharmila Chanu

Irom Sharmila Chanu is a human rights and civil rights activist from India, who is best known for her 16-year long hunger strike to protest against the Armed Forces (Special Powers) Act (AFSPA) in the Indian state of Manipur. Her activism brought attention to human rights abuses and the militarization of the region, and her speeches reflect her determination to bring an end to the AFSPA and to fight for justice for the people of Manipur.

One of her most inspiring speeches was delivered in 2006, while she was on hunger strike. In this speech, she spoke about the AFSPA and the devastating impact it has had on the people of Manipur. She said:

"I want to raise my voice against this act, which is a black law. I want the government to withdraw this act and provide justice to the people of Manipur."

She spoke about the human rights abuses committed by the military under the AFSPA, including extrajudicial killings, torture, and arbitrary detention. She also spoke about the impact of the military presence on the people of Manipur, which she said was causing immense suffering.

Another speech of hers, in her acceptance speech for the Gwangju Prize for Human Rights in 2016, she spoke about the importance of non-violent resistance and the power of human dignity. She said:

"I believe that non-violent resistance is the most effective weapon against repression and injustice. It is an assertion of human dignity and it is the people's power to reclaim their rights."

In her speech, she highlighted the importance of using non-violent resistance to bring about change, and spoke about the power of human dignity and the people's ability to reclaim their rights.

Throughout her activism, Irom Sharmila Chanu has been a powerful voice for human rights and civil rights in India. Her speeches were filled with determination, courage, and the message of non-violent resistance against injustice. Her remarkable resilience and her years of peaceful protest has gained her the respect and admiration of people globally and her fight for justice for the people of Manipur continues to be acknowledged, appreciated and used as a reference for other civil rights movements.

X

Tawakkol Karman

Tawakkol Karman is a journalist, politician, and human rights activist from Yemen, and is widely recognized for her role as a leader in the 2011 pro-democracy movement that led to the overthrow of President Ali Abdullah Saleh's regime. She is also the first Arab woman to receive the Nobel Peace Prize, which she received in 2011 for her work in non-violent struggle for the safety of women and for women's rights to full participation in peace-building work.

One of her most inspiring speeches was delivered in 2011, after receiving the Nobel Peace Prize. In her acceptance speech, she spoke about the importance of the youth in driving change and the role of women in peacebuilding. She said:

"Youth, who represent more than half of the Arab population, have been the driving force behind the Arab Spring. They have shown that they will not be denied their right to freedom, democracy and human dignity. They have shown that they are capable of leading their societies towards a better future."

She also spoke about the importance of women's participation in the peacebuilding process and in decision-making. She emphasized that the role of women in the Arab Spring and their participation in decision-making is a key step towards democracy and peace in Yemen and the region as a whole.

Another speech of hers, in her address at the United Nations General Assembly in 2011, she spoke about the urgent need for change in Yemen, and the importance of women's rights and democracy in the Arab world. She said:

"We, women of Yemen, have been subjected to double oppression, both as women and as citizens of an authoritarian regime. Therefore, our revolution is not only a revolution of young men and women who demand freedom, democracy, and social justice, but it is also a women's revolution that demands their rights, participation, and their role in decision-making."

In her speech, she highlighted the importance of the Arab Spring and the role of women in driving change, and she urged the international community to support the people of Yemen in their efforts to bring about democracy, peace, and human rights.

Throughout her activism, Tawakkol Karman has been a powerful voice for democracy, human rights, and women's rights in Yemen. Her speeches were filled with passion, determination, and a call for change. Her tireless efforts to promote human rights and democracy have earned her the respect and admiration of people all over the world, and her legacy continues to inspire generations of activists, fighting for their rights and the rights of their communities.

XI

Rigoberta Menchú

Rigoberta Menchú is a indigenous rights activist from Guatemala and a Nobel Peace Prize laureate. She is from the K'iche' Maya people and throughout her activism, she has been an outspoken advocate for the rights of indigenous people and a voice against poverty, injustice, and discrimination faced by her community and many indigenous people in the country and the Americas.

One of her most inspiring speeches was delivered in 1992 after receiving the Nobel Peace Prize. In her acceptance speech, she spoke about the importance of recognizing the rights of indigenous people, and the role of indigenous women in the struggle for social justice. She said:

"For us, the indigenous people, being a woman means carrying the most heavy load, the most heavy burden. It means that we have always had to fight harder, to fight more than men. And that is the reason why, for us, for our part, the struggle for indigenous rights is also the struggle for women's rights."

She also spoke about the importance of unity among indigenous people and the need to work together to bring about change. She emphasized the importance of indigenous knowledge and culture in the struggle for social justice, and the need to respect and value the contributions of indigenous people to society.

Another speech of hers, in her address to the United Nations Permanent Forum on Indigenous Issues in 2002, she spoke about the importance of the UN Declaration on the Rights of Indigenous Peoples and the need for its implementation. She said:

"We have waited 500 years for the United Nations to recognize us, the indigenous peoples of the world. It took 500 years of resistance, of struggle, of sacrifice, of hope. The Declaration is the first step towards a new world, a world in which all peoples are respected, a world in which all peoples have the right to live in dignity, a world in which all peoples have the right to self-determination."

In her speech, she highlighted the importance of the declaration, not only as a legal instrument, but also as an opportunity for indigenous people to assert their rights, and urged the international community to ensure its implementation.

Throughout her activism, Rigoberta Menchú has been a powerful voice for indigenous rights, and has fought tirelessly to promote the rights of indigenous people, particularly women and children. Her speeches were filled with passion, determination, and a call for change. Her legacy continues to inspire generations of activists, fighting for the rights of indigenous people, and her works and speeches continue to be referenced and studied as an important reference for the indigenous rights movement globally.

XII

Wangari Maathai

Wangari Maathai is remembered as an environmental and political activist who played a significant role in fighting for political, social, and environmental justice in Kenya. Born in Nyeri, Kenya in 1940, Maathai applied her knowledge of science to educate and empower communities to challenge economic and political marginalization. Over the course of three decades, Maathai worked tirelessly to stand up for the rights of women, engage communities in environmentalism, and promote grassroots democracy.

Maathai's inspiring work began in 1977 with the establishment of the Green Belt Movement which encouraged the planting of millions of trees throughout Kenya. This was a grassroots project that relied heavily on local knowledge and leadership, with Maathai providing her expertise as a scientist and educator. Later, in 1992 Maathai used this knowledge to found the National Environmental Management Authority which worked to promote environmental conservation and formed a powerful platform for environmental activism.

In parallel to her environmental activism, Maathai used her platform to speak on behalf of democracy. Her beliefs were based on the idea that the people at the grassroots level are the primary driving force in social and political transformation. She championed the cause of democratic governance, speaking out against corruption, environmental degradation, and clashes between tribal communities.

Maathai recognized the power of her own voice, and dedicated her life to voicing her opinions whether in her home country of Kenya or on the global stage. She travelled around the world, communicating her ideas at countless seminars, conferences and talks. This included a powerful speech at the 2004 UN World Environment Day, where she encouraged people to take action against the destruction of the environment, and an address to the United Nations General Assembly in 2004.

Maathai's life and activism ended in 2011, but her legacy remains an inspiration for all who care about human rights, compassion for nature, and campaigns for economic justice. Her work provides a model for future activists to follow and emphasizes the importance of environmental and political action as interconnected forces. Through her work, Maathai established herself as a leader and pioneer in the fight for global justice & environmental sustainability, and her dedication and commitment to the vision will remain a constant reminder of what is possible when one takes a stand.

※

XIII

Malala Yousafzai

Malala Yousafzai - "He Named Me Malala" speech, delivered at the United Nations in 2013.

Malala Yousafzai rose to international fame as a teenager after her fight against a Taliban attack that left her seriously injured. In 2012, at a time when many girls were prevented from attending school in Pakistan, Yousafzai defied the odds and used her voice to speak up for the right to education of girls everywhere. This fight was documented in the 2015 documentary He Named Me Malala, which sought to tell Yousafzai's story and explore the impact she had on other young women.

The major themes of the film was Yousafzai's fight for equality in the face of extraordinary adversity and her message of resilience. The film highlights the strength she found in her father's love and support, which was rooted in the Islamic values of justice, kindness and respect for women. This strength was reflected in her speech and the events she attended, where she spoke with passion and eloquence about her beliefs.

The film took a narrative-driven approach to exploring Yousafzai's story, as it followed her and her family as they navigated the aftermath of the Taliban attack. The film also presented Yousafzai's inner strength, her willingness to fight for what she believes in and her impact on other young women. Through interviews with Yousafzai and her family, He Named Me Malala provided the world with an intimate look into the life and the struggle of those affected by the Taliban's brutality.

Yousafzai's speech and activism were met with criticism and even death threats. However, her bravery was highlighted in the film and her resilience, compassion and commitment to speaking out against injustice — which was echoed in her speeches around the world — was inspiring to many. He Named Me Malala captured Yousafzai's determination to create a change and to be a voice for the voiceless all over the world.

The film's message and impact had an international reach, as young women were not only inspired to speak out in the face of injustice but also to pursue their dreams. Yousafzai's story gives a voice to those who don't have one, and He Named Me Malala serves as a valuable reminder of her bravery and accomplishments. In conclusion, Malala Yousafzai's story and her inspiring speeches and activism led the way for many young women to fight for justice.

XIV

Mother Teresa

Mother Teresa - "Anywhere and Everywhere" speech, delivered at the Nobel Peace Prize ceremony in 1979.

Mother Teresa, one of the most admired figures in the world, was known for her charitable works and her words that touched the hearts of many people. In her speech, "Anywhere and Everywhere", she delivered a powerful message about life, and how one should treat their fellow men and women no matter where they are and who they are.

Mother Teresa began her speech by emphasizing the need for kindness and understanding in the world, and how we should be respectful and humble no matter where we go. According to her, "We need love and tenderness, we need to forgive and forget". She believes that we should forgive and not hold onto our resentments and grudges. Mother Teresa's point was to emphasize the importance of unconditional love and forgiveness in order to create a better world.

Furthermore, she expressed that we should have a strong desire to help and care for our fellow human beings. She believes that we are all equal, no matter our backgrounds or beliefs, and that we should strive to treat everyone with respect. Her words of wisdom and strength echoed in the hearts of those present, reminding them of our obligations toward one another as human beings, regardless of race, gender, or class.

Throughout her speech, Mother Teresa also discussed the importance of always putting the wellbeing of others first. As she put it, "We should become instruments of peace and bring joy and happiness everywhere". She insists that we should never be content in the comfort of our own lives, but instead should reach out and offer support and help those in need.

As Mother Teresa concluded, she left the audience with the utmost respect for life, for each other, and for their roles in the world. She reminded them of the power of love and of its possibilities when it is shared with those who may be in desperate need. She emphasized that "We have to help one another and love one another" so that the world can become a better place with less sorrow and more understanding.

Mother Teresa spoke with passion, conviction and sincerity in her speech, which moved its audience to take a stand for what is right and to always remain humble and kind. Her 'Anywhere and Everywhere' speech serves as a reminder of how even the deepest kindness and compassion can be shared. Our acts of kindness and love are not only important for ourselves, but for the entire world.

XV
Hillary Clinton

Hillary Clinton is a former Secretary of State and the first woman to win a major party's presidential nomination in the United States. Throughout her career, she has been an advocate for women's rights, children's welfare and universal healthcare, and her speeches reflect her commitment to these issues and to public service.

One of her most inspiring speeches was delivered in 1995 at the Fourth World Conference on Women in Beijing, where she famously declared, "Women's rights are human rights." In her speech, Clinton emphasized the importance of women's rights and the need to recognize that discrimination against women is a human rights issue.

She said: "It is a violation of human rights when women are denied the right to plan their own families, and that includes being forced to have abortions or being sterilized against their will. It is a violation of human rights when baby girls are killed in the womb simply because they are girls. It is a violation of human rights when women are raped in armed conflict, and when rape is used as a weapon of war."

She spoke about the need for governments to take action to ensure that women's rights are protected and for the international community to work together to promote gender equality.

Another speech of hers, in her 2016 concession speech after losing the presidential election, she spoke about the importance of unity and the need to support the rights of all citizens, regardless of gender, race, religion, or sexual orientation.

She said:"We have still not shattered that highest and hardest glass ceiling, but some day, someone will and hopefully sooner than we might think right now."

She also spoke about the importance of continuing the fight for equality, and urged her supporters to stay involved in politics and to continue to work for change.

Throughout her career, Hillary Clinton has been a powerful voice for women's rights and has made significant contributions to the fight for gender equality. Her speeches were filled with passion, determination, and a call for change. Her historic campaign in 2016, as the first woman to win a major party nomination for president in the United States, has inspired millions of women and girls to pursue their dreams, and to break through the glass ceiling that still exists in many fields.

XVI
Emma Watson

Emma Watson UN Women Goodwill Ambassadorpowerful speeches on gender equality.

One of the most powerful speeches on gender equality was delivered at the United Nations in 2014 by the then-UN Women Goodwill Ambassador, Emma Watson. The speech focused on the idea of gender equality, which had been seen as a contentious issue around the world, especially as women continued to face discrimination in their daily lives. In the speech, Watson emphasized that gender equality is not just an issue that affects women, but one that affects everyone, regardless of gender, ethnicity, or religious beliefs.

Watson began her speech by noting that time is running out to make meaningful change. She acknowledged the work of other activists before her, like Malala Yousafzai, and also spoke about the opportunities for people around the world to come together and make progress towards gender equality. She then outlined her own commitment to the cause of gender equality and urged the audience to make their own commitments to the cause.

To illustrate her point, Watson spoke passionately about her own experiences as a woman. She discussed how she was constantly targeted by the media,criticizing her physical appearance rather than her accomplishments. This, she argued, is a symptom of a much broader problem, whereby women are often not judged for their talents but instead for their gender. To remedy this issue, Watson urged people to join her in supporting gender equality.

In order to make effective change, Watson argued, people must understand the complexity of gender equality. She highlighted the need to change traditional gender roles and challenge ingrained stereotypes. To further her point, Watson spoke of the importance of education in creating a culture that prioritized gender equality. She argued that education is necessary for creating informed citizens who can fight for gender equality, thus improving the lives of women worldwide.

Finally, Watson closed her speech with a call to action. She asked the audience to make their own commitment to the cause by signing the UN's HeForShe campaign, which aimed to get men and boys around the world involved in the fight for gender equality. By signing the campaign, they would be showing their support and helping to build a gender-equal world.

Ultimately, Watson's speech on gender equality was quite inspiring. It highlighted the deeply rooted issues facing women across the world, while also emphasizing the need to take action. By outlining her own commitment and calling on people to make their own, she demonstrated the power of individuals to effect change. Thanks to her powerful words and inspiring message, Emma Watson's speech on gender equality at the UN was a landmark moment in the fight for equal rights for women.

XVII
Chimamanda Ngozi Adichie

Chimamanda Ngozi Adichie is a novelist and feminist writer from Nigeria. Her TED talk "We Should All Be Feminists" has been widely popular and influential, and it was later transformed into a book. Throughout her work, she has been a vocal advocate for gender equality and women's rights, and her speeches reflect her passion for these issues.

One of her most inspiring speeches was delivered during her TED talk "We Should All Be Feminists" in 2012. In her talk, she spoke about the limitations of the traditional definition of feminism and the need for a more inclusive and intersectional understanding of the term. She said:

"We must raise our daughters differently. We must also raise our sons differently. ...We do a great disservice to boys in how we raise them. We stifle the humanity of boys. We define masculinity in a very narrow way. Masculinity is a hard, small cage, and we put boys inside this cage."

She emphasized that feminism is not about demonizing men, but about creating a more equal society where men and women can be themselves without the constraints of restrictive gender roles. She advocated for raising both girls and boys differently to break the cycles of gender stereotype.

Another speech of hers, in her "The Danger of a Single Story" TED talk in 2009, she spoke about the importance of multiple perspectives and the dangers of a single story.

She said:"The single story creates stereotypes, and the problem with stereotypes is not that they are untrue, but that they are incomplete. They make one story become the only story."

In her speech, she spoke about how a single story can create an incomplete picture of a person, a community, or a culture and how it can lead to misunderstanding and a lack of empathy. She urged her audience to seek out multiple perspectives and to question their own assumptions.

Throughout her work, Chimamanda Ngozi Adichie has been a powerful voice for gender equality and women's rights. Her speeches were filled with insight, passion and a call for change. Her TED talk "We Should All Be Feminists" was considered a cultural phenomenon and has been widely popular and influential, it has provided an accessible and powerful introduction to feminist theory and it continues to inspire and educate people on the importance of equality and intersectionality.

XVIII

Isabel Allende

Isabel Allende is a Chilean-American author and feminist, her speeches have advocated for women's rights, equality and have touched on cultural, political, and personal issues. Throughout her career, she has been an outspoken advocate for women's rights and equality, and her speeches reflect her passion for these issues.

One of her most inspiring speeches was delivered in 2014 at the Women in the World Summit, where she spoke about the importance of women's empowerment and the role of women in shaping the future.

She said: "Women have always been the backbone of society, we are the ones that hold families and communities together. We are the ones that make the future, we must be equal partners in decision-making and in shaping the world."

She spoke about the importance of education for girls, and about the need for women to have equal access to opportunities, resources, and power. She also urged women to support each other and to lift each other up, saying "A woman alone can be attacked and diminished, but together we are formidable."

Another speech of hers, in her acceptance speech for the National Book Award for Fiction for her book "In the Midst of Winter" in 2018, she spoke about the importance of storytelling and its power to connect people across cultures and borders.

She said: "Stories are a way to connect with others, to understand their struggles and triumphs, to see the world through different eyes. They are a bridge that unites us and makes us feel less alone. Stories give voice to the voiceless and make the invisible visible."

Allende emphasized the importance of using literature as a tool for social change and to give a voice to marginalized communities. She also highlighted the power of storytelling to bring people together and to create empathy and understanding.

Allende's speeches reflect her deep commitment to women's rights and equality, and her belief in the power of women to shape the future. She is an advocate for education and access to opportunities for girls and women, and encourages women to support each other in the pursuit of equality. Through her speeches, she also emphasizes the power of storytelling and literature to connect people and bring about social change. Her speeches are a powerful reminder of the importance of working towards gender equality and the role of women in shaping the future.

Isabel Allende has used her platform as an author and a public figure to advocate for women's rights and equality, her speeches are empowering and inspiring as they reflect her own dedication and contributions to a gender-equal society. Her books give voice to the voiceless, shines light to the invisible, and creates a narrative for a gender-equal future.

XIX

Mary Robinson

Mary Robinson is a trailblazer in both politics and human rights. As the first female President of Ireland, she broke barriers and served as a role model for women in politics. Throughout her career, Robinson has been a powerful advocate for human rights and climate change, using her platform to raise awareness and inspire action on these critical issues.

In her speeches, Robinson often highlights the interconnectedness of human rights and climate change, emphasizing the ways in which climate change disproportionately affects marginalized communities and threatens the most basic human rights, such as the right to life and the right to food.

For example, In a speech at the UN Climate Action Summit in 2019, Robinson said, "Climate change is a human rights crisis. It undermines the rights of present and future generations to life, to health, to food and water, to housing, to work, to culture and to self-determination. Climate change is also a threat multiplier, exacerbating existing inequalities, discrimination and poverty."

Robinson also stresses the urgency of action on climate change, noting that the window for meaningful action is rapidly closing. In her speeches, she calls on individuals, governments, and organizations to take bold and immediate steps to address the crisis and build a more just and sustainable future.

In addition, Robinson has always been an advocate for gender equality, in a speech at the High-Level Meeting on the Elimination and Prevention of all Forms of Violence Against Women and Girls in 2015, She stated "Gender equality is both a fundamental human right and a key driver of sustainable development. The denial of women's rights to equality and participation leads to increased poverty, underdevelopment and insecurity."

Mary Robinson's speeches are powerful and inspiring, drawing attention to the critical issues of human rights and climate change and calling for immediate action to address them. Her speeches continue to inspire people around the world to take action to build a more just and sustainable future.

Other Books Of The Author

1. The Moments When I Met God
2. Kashiyile Theertha Pathangal
3. GURU GYAN VANI
4. Abhiprerak Gita
5. ASSI SE JAIN GHAT TAK
6. Hopelessness of Arjuna
7. The Soul and It's True Nature
8. Sense of Action (Karma)
9. Action through Wisdom
10. Action through Wisdom
11. THEORY AND PRACTICAL OF EVERY ACTION
12. LOGICAL UNDERSTANDING OF THE SUPREME
13. THE IMPERISHABLE SUPREME
14. Yatra Nishadraj se Hanuman Ghat Tak
15. Yatra Karnatak Ghat se Raja Ghat Tak
16. Yatra Pandey Ghat se Prayagraj Ghat Tak
17. Yatra Ranjendra Prasad Ghat se Dattatreya Ghat Tak
18. YaatraSindhiya Ghat se Gwaliar Ghat Tak
19. Yatra Mangala Gauri Ghat se Hanuman Gadhi Ghat Tak
20. Yatra Gaay Ghat Se Nishad Ghat Tak
21. MAA GANGA, GHATEN EVM UTSAV
22. Ganga Arti Dev Deepavali evam Any Utsav
23. Potentials of Digitalized India
24. VEDIC CONSCIOUSNESS
25. A Brief Introduction to Vedic Science
26. Kashi ke Barah Jyotirling
27. IMPACT OF MOTIVATION
28. Let's have a Milky Way Journey
29. Color Therapy in a Nutshell

30. Rigveda in a Nutshell
31. Yajurveda in a Nutshell
32. Samveda in a Nutshell
33. Atharva Veda in a Nutshell
34. Ayushman Bhava - Ayurveda
35. Srimad Bhagavad Gita and Upanishad Connection
36. Srimad Bhagavad Gita - an attempt to summarize each chapter.
37. Facts and Impact of Nakshatra
38. Astro Gems - NAVARATNA
39. Ekadashi - A Concise Overview
40. A Concise View of Hanuman Chalisa
41. Inspirational Gita
42. Nakshatraranyam
43. Summary of 18 Mahapuranas
44. Synopsis of 18 Upa Puranas
45. Rigvediya Upanishads
46. Shukla Yajurvediya Upanishads
47. Krishna Yajurvediya Upanishads
48. Samavediya Upanishads
49. Atharvavediya Upanishads
50. The Seven Great Sages
51. From Rocket Scientist to President Dr. APJ Abdul Kalam
52. The Visionary's Voice - Quotes of Dr. APJ Abdul Kalam
53. The Wisdom of Swami Vivekananda: Insights and Inspiration from a Legendary Spiritual Teacher
54. Ayurvedic Remedies from the Garden
55. Sages and Seers
56. Rising Strong – Motivational Stories of Women
57. Beyond Flames -Mystery stories of Funeral Ghat Manikarnika
58. **The Origins of Tulsi: A Look at the Mythological Roots of the Plant"**

59. "The Holistic Cow: A Look at the Physical, Spiritual, and Cultural Importance of Cows in India"

60. Five Elements

ॐ

Contact

DR. JAGADEESH PILLAI

PhD in Vedic Science

Four Times Guinness World Record Holder

Winner of Mahatma Gandhi Vishwa Shanti Puraskar and
Global Peace Ambassador

Gemology, Astro & Vastu Consultant - Spiritual Counselor

Consultant for designing World Record Ideas

Efficient Tarot Card Reader

9839093003

myrichindia@gmail.com

drjagadeeshpillai@facebook

drjagadeeshpillai@instagram

jagadeeshpillai@youtube

www. JAGADEESHPILLAI.com

|| LOKAHA SAMASTHAHA SUKHINO BHAVANTU ||

• 55 •